SINGLE WITH GOD

Why am I still single?

MIKE SZCZESNY

LEONINE PUBLISHERS
PHOENIX, ARIZONA

Published by

Leonine Publishers LLC
Phoenix, Arizona, USA

ISBN-13: 978-1-942190-37-0
Library of Congress Control Number: 2017955352

Printed in the United States of America
10 9 8 7 6 5 4 3 2 1

Visit us online at www.leoninepublishers.com
For more information: info@leoninepublishers.com

"The word of the Lord said to me,
Before I formed you in the womb, I knew you,
before you were born I dedicated you,
a prophet to the nations I appointed you."
~ Jeremiah 1:4-5

"He who trusts in himself is lost.
He who trusts in God can do all things."
~ St. Alphonsus Liguori

CONTENTS

Introduction 1

Seeing Through the Eyes of a Child 3

The Adventure Begins 5

Having a Sporting Chance 7

Peer Pressure and Flat Hopes 9

Falling Short 10

A Prescription for Success 12

Prom-ising Hopes 13

A Prescription for Failure 15

Making an Accounting of My Career 16

Feeling Singled Out 18

Do You Want Purpose and Fries With That? 19

A Learning Experience 20

A Singularly Moving Prayer 24

Flying Solo 25

Getting Into the Spirit of Things 27

A Dance Encounter With Her 28

A Safari So Good 30

There Is No Place Like a Spiritual Home 31

Blurred Vision 32

Her Face That Launched 1000 Tears 34

Easy as π 36

To My Surprise! 38

Fasten Your Seat Belts 39

"I'll Take Vocations for $200, Alex..." 40

Getting On board God's Providence Express 43

God, Is That What You Do? 44

A Single-minded Idea 45

Proceed With Caution:
Detours, Obstacles (and Ironies) Ahead 47

What Is a Single Person to Do? 50

Idol Thoughts About Marriage and Singleness 52

Looking Out From God's Castle 53

Better Blessings and Gifts 55

Relationships: A Match Made in Heaven 55

What Does the Old Testament Say
About Singleness? 56

What Does the New Testament Say
About Singleness? 60

Final Thoughts 63

Note from the author 65

About the author 65

INTRODUCTION

1982: It's Going to Be a Bumpy Ride....

Richard and I walked quickly toward the front entrance of the wooden roller-coaster ride at AstroWorld amusement park. Along with many others, we arrived at the park just before 10:00 am, the time the park opened. Today was going to be another very humid and sunny July day. Having a light, fair skin tone, I easily get sunburned. Because of this I needed to wear a baseball cap and use suntan lotion.

We finally arrived at the entrance to the Texas Cyclone roller-coaster attraction. We passed through the maze of aisles, waiting to get onto the roller coaster. As we got closer to the departure point, we heard "clacking" and "whooshing" noises. The clacking noises became louder as we saw the train of roller-coaster cars slowly move up to the highest point of the track. Then shortly after, we heard the loud whoosh of another train of roller-coaster cars slowing down as it approached its stop. The attendant on hand pressed the button to engage the braking system.

The returning roller-coaster cars came to a complete stop for the next group of passengers. It was finally our turn to get into the coaster cars. We got in and buckled ourselves in our seats. The protective steel shoulder bar automatically moved up in place against our chests. In a few minutes, we were going to ride.

Richard said to me, "You better make sure you hold on to your hat and sunglasses."

I said, "Yea, I am holding them tight." We were ready to start. As we slowly moved up the track, the clacking noises

1

surrounded us. We finally reached the top and then began a fast descent down the track.

A short two minutes later, we were coming to the end of our ride. We heard the whoosh sounds as the roller coaster began to slow down, returning where we started. As we came to a complete stop, the shoulder bar automatically moved forward. Immediately everyone exited their seats. Upon getting up, I saw a splattering of white lotion inside my front right pocket.

I said, "I didn't see that coming…"

CHAPTER 1
SEEING THROUGH THE EYES OF A CHILD

1966: The Man With the Cape

There were a lot people in the building. We all sat down. I turned around and looked up at the windows. They were pretty, with colors of blue, yellow, and brown.

"Mike," my mom looked at me, "sit down. They're going to be starting pretty soon."

"OK, Mommy," I said, sitting back down, but I still looked at the windows. They showed people with circles around their heads. I also saw a sheep. I heard music. Then we had to stand up and sit down. Later, I saw the man up front behind a large table. He was holding up a shiny gold cup. He was also wearing a large sheet. No. It was a cape.

I cried out, "Batman!"

My mom looked at me. I knew that she was mad.

"Shh," she said. She already told me to be quiet and she repeated, "You need to be quiet when we are in church!" The way she looked at me, I knew I was in trouble like the Joker.

1967: My Eyes Open

"Jingle bells, jingle bells, jingle all the way…" The sound of Christmas carols filled the air.

It was a mild 68 degrees in the Mission Hills subdivision in the San Fernando Valley area of Los Angeles. Fog blanketed the neighborhood.

* * *

It was Christmas Eve and we just finished opening the gifts. My mom and dad were sitting on the carpet at the foot of the tree, watching me and my brother playing with our gifts from Santa. My brother was pushing his Hot Wheels car on the racetrack. I was playing with my Rock 'Em Sock 'Em Robots. I kept pushing down the buttons to knock the other robot's head upwards.

* * *

I then went back to the kitchen to get some more cookies. Next to the cookies, there was a small snow globe. I shook it, to make the snow fall on the little log cabin inside the globe. There were two small figures of people holding hands, walking to the log cabin. The snow was falling all over the place. I always wondered what it would be like in a real snow storm.

"Look at Mike," my dad said to my mom, "he is very curious looking into that snow globe. They've never seen snow."

My mom said, "You're right, since they were both born here in Los Angeles. Personally, I don't miss it at all."

My mom and dad were both born and raised in Erie, in northwest Pennsylvania, right off of Lake Erie. Mom and Dad moved to Los Angeles to find better weather and job prospects. I couldn't keep my eyes off that snow globe. I don't know what it was. I saw them from the outside looking in.

CHAPTER 2
THE ADVENTURE BEGINS

I could see Mom in the hallway. She said, "Mike and Donny, get ready to go to bed. Get into your pajamas. Dad and I want to talk to you tonight before you go to bed."

My brother and I got into our pajamas and jumped into our beds. Both Mom and Dad came into our bedroom and sat down on our beds.

Dad first spoke, "Kids, Mom and I have something to tell you. Pretty soon we are going to be moving to a new place in another state. We are going to Houston, Texas. So, it is going to be a long trip in our car."

I asked, "Is it going to be like when we went to Aunt Sophie's house?"

Dad said, "No, it's going to be much longer than that. We will be driving all day in the car for two days." Mom and Dad both looked at us, to see how we would react to this.

As Mom noticed that Don and I were looking at each other, she said, "We are going take all of our things and put it all in a large moving truck."

Dad added, "You had a lot of fun at Aunt Sophie's, didn't you?

Don and I shouted, "Yea, that was a lot of fun."

Then Dad said, "Think of this as a big adventure. You are going to meet new people and make new friends." Mom and Dad left our room and turned off the light.

I wondered, as I fluffed up my pillow, "Maybe there will be snow."

1969: At First Blush

"Everybody settle down now. You need to get quiet. We are going to be starting class now," our teacher said to us. Our first-grade teacher was a very nice young woman. She did sometimes get upset, when we talked too much. But other than that, we all liked having her as our teacher. Our classroom was located on one side of the hallway next to the bus loading zone. As the front wall was lined with a series of frosted window planes, one could vaguely see the teacher and students inside the classroom, when walking through this hallway. A large chalkboard covered the bulk of the back wall. The remaining walls were lined with posters, shelves, and school supplies. Instead of small seats, the classroom contained several large tables where six students sat facing each other. Some of the kids needed to turn around when the teacher wanted everyone's attention.

* * *

Tracy was seated across from me, between myself and the teacher standing at the front of the class. One day before class started, our table was just talking and joking around. Class was going to be starting pretty soon.

"Mike likes Tracy!" said Davey. He said this with a big grin on his face, then laughed.

"No, I don't," I quickly replied. I was feeling embarrassed and getting red in my face.

"Yes, you do," Davey said.

Of course, he was right. I liked Tracy. I had often glanced at Tracy, when I should have been paying attention to the teacher. I didn't know if she liked me. I was too afraid to find out. They say school is where you learned things. I learned that I liked Tracy.

CHAPTER 3
HAVING A SPORTING CHANCE

Striking Out

It was that time again to begin another season of Little League baseball. This was to be my fourth year, after playing one year in the pee wee league division and two years in the minor league division. My little brother, a year younger than me, also played last season in the minor league division. I was hoping this year that I would make it to the major league. My brother made it to the major league, but I remained in the minors. I struck out on my chance to keep up with my brother.

This Is Going to Be a Slam Dunk

The gym was a chamber of voices, bounces, steps, and screeches, occurring all at once. Basketballs could be heard bouncing all over the wood-lined court. Players were running back and forth the length of the course, stretching and loosening up for the scrimmage game. At the sideline near the bleachers, the coach was talking to me and some of the other players.

The coach was talking about last week's game, which our team won against our nearby high school rival. This game was for the district conference championship. Our team, in a hard-fought contest, edged out our rival in the final seconds by three points. As our team had won district, it was determined that the final scheduled game of the season was cancelled.

Our team was now in preparation to compete in inter–district playoffs. Our coach decided that our team would have a scrimmage game, instead of a normal practice session. As custom with the end of the season, team photos would also be taken in the gym. At the corner of the gym, the school photography staff was setting up their equipment. Once our team was finished with these team photos, we would begin our scrimmage game.

The coach finished talking with us. As we were leaving to warm up, the coach called me back, wanting to briefly talk with me in private.

The coach mentioned that he was very proud of my improvement this year, playing center.

"If you keep this up, practicing and playing hard, you can go far in basketball in high school and in college."

"Coach," I responded, "thanks for the kind words."

One of the photography staff visited the coach and told him that they were ready for the photo session.

The coach acknowledged this and said, "Guys, stop what you're doing. They are ready to begin to shoot the photos."

We all headed to the corner of the gym next to the wall. The photographers were to take an individual photo of each player and take a group photo. The coach then added, "When they're done taking picture, we will start our practice."

* * *

When my team lined up together for the group photo, I was the tallest player on my team at six foot two, playing the center position. My height helped me to have a successful year, leading to our district championship.

I can't wait to see how tall I am when I am going to be in high school. There is no stopping me now! This is going to be a slam dunk.

CHAPTER 4

PEER PRESSURE AND FLAT HOPES

My Peers and Then the Tears

"Mom, I need to head out. My friends are outside waiting for me," I said as I closed the door.

It was almost the end of the school year in eighth grade. The junior high was right next to our neighborhood. So, we only had to walk three streets down through our subdivision to get to school. As we were walking down the street, we saw the same classmate walking hand in hand with his girlfriend every morning.

I was looking at them.

"Mike, did you hear what I said?" my friend asked.

"What?" I turned around to my friend. "What did you say?"

He must have said something to me, but I didn't pay attention to him. It seems that I was lost in thought, again looking at those two holding hands. The year was rapidly coming to an end. I reflected back on my experiences in school for the last three years. A flood of memories came to mind, memories of junior high school. But there were also the images of those situations that I had never experienced.

The boys carrying their girlfriends' books....

The boys and girls kissing each other in the hallway...

The popular jock eating lunch with his girlfriend...

The boys and girls holding each others' hand in the school hallway.

I had seen these images so many times, but still on the outside looking in.

CHAPTER 5
FALLING SHORT

Being Cut Down to Size

The basketball season was winding down. Instead of playing center position on the freshman team, I played the forward position for the whole season. I played center in only a limited capacity that season. It was an eye-opening experience for me, being a much more difficult season.

I was not one of the tallest basketball players anymore. I had stopped growing. I was still the same size as I was in junior high. It was more difficult to score points and make assists. I was not as quick as the others. It was becoming more difficult to compete with the better players on the court. I just couldn't keep up with them.

Several months later I started my sophomore year. I was looking forward to my next season playing basketball. Hopefully, the practice, drills, physical conditioning, and weightlifting would help prepare me for the next season.

* * *

"Come on, Mike," the coach said to me, "you need it pick it up."

The coach had often said this to me when I was falling behind, trying to keep up, and catching my breath. I did not want to face the fact that maybe I couldn't cut it anymore. This also cut down my hopes for a future basketball career.

* * *

As the season progressed, I found myself being second string, sitting on the bench for most of the season. I was frustrated, realizing that I wasn't improving as much as I wanted or needed. I was not getting any better. This really began to weigh heavily on my mind. Things were not going to change for me. I had to make a decision.

One afternoon before basketball practice, I was heading toward the coach's office. Practice had not yet started and the coach was in his office taking care of some paper work. I was still in my normal school clothes.

"Coach, got a minute? I need to talk to you," I said.

"Sure, Mike. What's on your mind?" the coach answered back.

"I have been thinking about this a lot." I was getting upset, almost crying. "I have decided to quit basketball. It's now just so hard for me to keep up. I am spending a lot of time on the bench. It is just not fun anymore."

I was now getting more upset, thinking that I would be letting the coach down.

"Mike, I know that you been trying real hard out there and giving all you can."

I guess I didn't expect to hear this from my coach. Instead of being disappointed in me, the coach looked at me with concern and understanding.

"Are you sure you want to do this?" he asked me.

I immediately responded, "Yes, I think this would be best for me."

"OK," my coach said. "I will let the team know," he added, as headed out of the office into the gym to start practice.

I saw the writing on the court; I was not going to be that star basketball player.

Instead of returning to the locker room, I sat at a table in the cafeteria. The gym and locker room were located near the cafeteria. In fact, I was looking straight ahead at the gym door, thinking of all the times I headed to the locker room. I remember my dad saying life is an adventure. But I really did not expect this detour.

As I was sitting alone and quiet, it just then dawned on me that I had always sat with my teammates here for lunch.

"Oh my God, what are my friends going to think? What are they going to say?"

I was dreading coming to lunch tomorrow!

That's a Foul!

My little brother, in his sophomore year, earned a position on the varsity basketball team. It was not fair!

CHAPTER 6
A PRESCRIPTION FOR SUCCESS

"Mike, have you given some thought about what you want to do with your life?" my Dad asked me one Saturday afternoon.

"Yea, I have been thinking about this a lot. I am thinking about going into pharmacy There will always be a need for people to take medicine. I just think that would be a good way to help."

My dad said, "Yes, I think that is a good choice, since we have a college of pharmacy in town."

I knew the best was yet to come for me. I had a prescription for success!

CHAPTER 7
PROM-ISING HOPES

"Mike, have you thought about whom you are going ask out for the prom?" my friend asked me.

"No, I haven't just yet. I will soon," I said, not having a clue about this.

I wanted to to change the subject. How can I avoid talking about this? However, as the prom was coming up in a few weeks, it was impossible not to. Throughout junior high and even high school, I never had even one girlfriend.

Why! Why, wasn't there anyone ever interested in me? I felt that I had lost out having these experiences. Whom am I going to ask out? Will I be able to find someone? I felt again like that outsider looking in.

She Took My Heart at the Ballgame

"Are you going to your brother's baseball game? It's at 4:00 pm this afternoon," my mom told me.

"Yea, I think so. I don't have to go to work tonight," I answered.

Baseball season was normally during the latter part of the school year. My brother Don, in addition to becoming a skilled basketball player, also played on the varsity baseball team. He played third base.

Our family arrived at the high school baseball field. We found a place to sit in the bleachers. Later more spectators and fans trickled in, taking their seats in anticipation of this game against a nearby, rival high school. A large crowd was anticipated to be present to watch this important game.

* * *

The game was expected to start in a few minutes. The home team took the field, going through warm ups in preparation for the game. As I watched them on the field, I noticed a young woman sit next to me at the end of the bleachers. There she was. I had never seen someone as beautiful as she was. I found the nerve to talk to her. We struck up a conversation, telling each other about ourselves. Her name was Amy.

"My brother, out there on the field, plays third base," I said to Amy, as the game was about to start. Although I was still somewhat envious of my brother's athletic abilities, at least she was interested in talking to me.

Amy looked at me and responded, "How exciting. I love baseball."

As we further talked, I learned that she was a sophomore, class of 1984. I told her that I was in the class of 1981 and I was attending college. I was really taken with Amy. I found myself wanting more to talk with her, rather than watching my brother play. To be honest, I was never much of a baseball fan. In our conversation, I happened to find the courage to ask Amy if she was interested in going out. I had learned that she wasn't seeing someone at this time.

"Amy, I was wondering if you would be interested in going out sometime. I don't know…maybe something like a movie?" I looked at her.

Amy responded with a slight smile and said, "Mike, I would like that."

She gave me her number. We both watched the game. During this time we exchanged small talk and quick side glances at each other. Later, our school team won the game and the fans loudly cheered. Everyone began to leave. As Amy was leaving, we shared a few silent seconds, smiling at each other. I waved to her as she left. I could hardly believe what just happened! Someone actually wanted to be with me! I actually made a hit with her.

* * *

We did go out once to the movies. However, we both were later finding it difficult to find time together, as we were both busy with school and other activities. I was busy with school and work. Amy was busy with school and cheerleading. I again tried to see if we could go out. Eventually, this situation never led to the next date. I later found out that she was dating a junior in high school. I did not know what to think. I was devastated. Amy had stolen my heart, but I struck out again in love.

CHAPTER 8
A PRESCRIPTION FOR FAILURE

1984-1986

I finally finished taking all my prerequisite classes, attended by large numbers of students of various majors. It was often difficult making friendships when you find yourself seated next to a new person each class. Now I was going to look forward to taking classes more directly related to my major.

I was able to make some new friends in class. It was nice to finally share a common goal with others, which was to graduate in pharmacy. I looked forward to these friendships in the years to come.

* * *

A Cruel Irony

However, things did not go as well as I had hoped. I found myself struggling in several of my classes, struggling to make passing grades. I eventually had to repeat some courses. Yet, my friends were moving forward, while I was falling behind.

* * *

As I continued my studies, I further struggled, having to repeat more classes. So, I fell further behind. I knew that pharmacy was a difficult major, but I thought I could succeed. I did not want to face the fact that I would fail in this career path, because I did not want to start over.

* * *

Then came the next semester. I managed to spectacularly fail three courses, further lowering my grade point average. As a result, I was placed on academic suspension.

I thought about changing my major, but I didn't want to start all over again. But the cruel irony was that, despite my best efforts, I eventually had to start over again. I spent all those years studying, and I had nothing to show for it. What was I going to do now? I had never felt so miserable. Why did this happen to me!

CHAPTER 9
MAKING AN ACCOUNTING OF MY CAREER

So I was put on academic suspension from college. What was I supposed to do now? I asked myself this for a long time. From my correspondence with college faculty, I learned that I could appeal my suspension. I also was able to find a job working in a pharmacy. Hopefully, this would help in my effort to get back to school. About a year and a half later, I learned that my appeal was declined. What was I to do now?

I had to make a decision. I just couldn't believe that I spent so many years pursuing pharmacy, but with nothing to show for it, except a low GPA.

Fortunately, I later found out that I was able to get back to school and pursue an accounting degree. About four years later, I was able to graduate with my bachelor's degree! Although it was often difficult not to dwell on the past, I was so thankful that I had finally succeeded. Yes, I was proud about what I had accomplished. Yet, some things had never changed for me.

* * *

During one semester, I carpooled to school with two college girls. I was interested in one of these persons. However, she was not interested in me.

A year later, I found a study partner in my finance class. We became friends, and I was interested in dating her. But, again, she was not interested in me. I just couldn't account for all the loneliness in life. It just didn't add up!

* * *

1986

I joined a Christian singles, young adult group in my area of town. This group provided fellowship for singles through social, sport, spiritual, and service activities. I was looking forward to getting involved with this group. It was going to be nice to make new friends. And perhaps, I would finally find someone special.

CHAPTER 10
FEELING SINGLED OUT

1991

This was a bittersweet time in my life, with conflicting emotions. One the one hand, I was thankful and grateful for obtaining my accounting degree. But, I was still miserable and lonely. *Am I ever going to find someone?*

Knowing that I was not alone in my situation was very comforting for me. The vast majority of these singles in the group were establishing their careers. And here I was having to start over again in my career, making my dating situation even more complicated.

The more time I was involved with this group, I realized that I had become one of the older members. Was I ever going to find that special someone? Will it ever happen to me? I found many friends. But not that special person to spend my life with! *Why is this happening to me? Why is it so hard for me to find that special someone?*

I remember my dad saying, "You will find that special person in life." *Where is she?*

I was still on the outside looking in, as several of my friends were able to find that special person.

O Brother! Why Can't It Be Me!

My brother got married in 1991 in Louisiana. I was happy for him, but inside it really hurt.

CHAPTER 11
DO YOU WANT PURPOSE AND
FRIES WITH THAT?

It just never ended. It was the same old thing. I had gone to so many events, I lost count. I met new people and made new friends. But nothing happened. I was still alone and lonely. I just felt empty. It was always weighing heavily on my mind. I needed a distraction.

* * *

Fortunately, our group sponsored an event to go to AstroWorld, the amusement park in town, near the Astrodome. Well, I was going. At least, I was going to have some fun that day. We were scheduled to meet at 10:00 am, Saturday morning at McDonalds. From there we were carpooling to the amusement park. So I decided to get to the McDonalds a little early at 9:30 to get some breakfast. Afterwards, I sat down in a booth. As I was eating, I saw others come inside to place their orders. My friend Dave, with his food, came and sat at my table.

"Mike," Dave said, as he sat across from me in the booth I was sitting at. "I'm glad that I ran into you. I would like to ask you something."

"Hi, Dave. OK," I answered. I was wondering what he was going to say.

He said, "I was wondering if you would be interested in helping out with the religious education program at Prince of Peace church? They are looking for RE teachers and assistants. I am teaching a ninth-grade RE class."

To be honest, I wasn't really familiar with teaching religion. I said, "I don't know… I have really never done any teaching. I am an accountant. I really don't know too much about the Bible or church stuff. I have to think about it."

19

Dave said, "That's OK. It's really not that important to know how to teach. I also didn't have any teaching experience. I am a chemical engineer. We will begin our next year teaching this fall in September. If you are interested, just contact the RE office at Prince of Peace."

* * *

We couldn't have picked a better day to go to the amusement part. It was expected to be sunny and clear all day. I was looking forward to this day. This would be a good distraction for me, at least for one day. I thoroughly enjoyed myself and being with friends at AstroWorld, just having fun.

* * *

A few days later I really thought about what Dave had said to me. To be honest, I was miserable, frustrated, and discouraged from all the stuff I had been dealing with in my life. Perhaps this would be a good distraction for me, to focus on something else. So I made a decision to take up Dave's offer to help out at the church.

Yes, I am going to do this. I need the distraction for a little while.

CHAPTER 12
A LEARNING EXPERIENCE

Several days later I contacted my parish, letting them know I would be interested in helping out with the high school RE program. I was contacted and later assigned to be an assistant for a ninth-grade class on Sunday nights. Our first class would be starting the next month in September. I wasn't exactly sure what I was getting into. I was encouraged to attend the RE teacher orientation sessions to get acquainted with the teacher in our class. Her name was Lisa.

"I'm glad that you're going to help out this fall teaching. I am looking forward to teaching again this session," Lisa said. Evidently, Lisa already had experience teaching high school.

I looked at Lisa and said, "I haven't taught before. I really do not know too much about religion."

Lisa, trying to reassure me, answered, "Don't worry about it. You really do not need to have any experience. Just follow my lead and you'll be alright." She further added, "We have our lesson plans. All we need to do is just follow these lesson plans."

I said, "Now I will learn how to become a teacher."

* * *

I later attended a series of RE teacher workshops and elective classes with Lisa in preparation for our first class in September. The classes were intended to supplement the faith and provide the resources for the RE teachers for the upcoming year. During the last workshop, Lisa and I received our lesson plans for our weekly Sunday night ninth-grade RE sessions. We decided to meet together Monday nights to prepare our lesson plans for the following Sunday's class.

"Lisa, I really don't know too much about this material for this class."

She looked at me with a slight grin and said, "That's the neat thing about teaching this class. The kids in the classroom aren't the only students. We are also learning it as we prepare and teach the material."

I thought about what she said. I said, "That makes sense. I never thought about it that way."

So now I am going to learn about my faith.

It was time for our first RE class. It was hectic at first, since this was the first class. Lisa mentioned that the kids would settle down as they attend more sessions. Lisa suggested I follow her lead. Then with a few classes, Lisa and I would get in a routine when leading the class. When I first decided to help out, I really did not know what to expect. Even some of the kids started to ask questions about their faith. I was glad Lisa was there to answer the questions. I learned that I couldn't answer the questions. I also learned that I didn't know much about my faith.

You're on Deck

About a month later, I received a call from the assistant RE director at church. He said, "Mike, Lisa said she was not going to make it to class."

"What!" I immediately responded. "What do you mean?"

He answered, "Lisa was spending this weekend in Austin, and she is having car trouble. She is stuck in Austin. So you need to lead the class tonight."

Upon hanging up the phone, I didn't say anything for a few moments. I began to feel a little uneasy. *I hope I can do this!*

On the bright side, we had already planned our lesson this past Monday. The Boy Scouts had it right. Be prepared. I got to the classroom early to prepare for class. I taught the lesson plan. It was a little hectic, facing a few curve balls. But my prayers helped prepare me to step up to the plate.

1994: You Give and You Receive

It was the final RE class for the year. Lisa and I just finished our final class. Now it was time for us to gather in our prayer circle for the very last time.

Lisa said, "Well, this is it. Mike and I both enjoyed having you all here in this class. We hope you were able to get something out this class. We wish you all the very best in the future."

We said our final prayers, and the class officially ended. As the students were leaving the classroom, Lisa and I talked for a little while.

Lisa said, "Mike, I really appreciated your help this year. I really couldn't have done this without you."

We both briefly talked about the service projects our class participated in. At Halloween, our class ran a booth at the carnival to raise money for the food ministry. At Thanksgiving, our students did a scavenger hunt to collect canned goods for the food pantry. And at Christmas, our class adopted and provided gifts to a needy family.

I said, "That was a lot of fun. I was glad to help."

As we were tidying and cleaning up the room, Lisa and I briefly hugged. We turned off the lights and went our separate ways. As I was heading to my car, I reflected over what we did this past year.

I thought to myself, "Yes. It was a lot fun. It felt good doing this. I'm not exactly sure why. But I really enjoyed it."

I really did get something from doing this.

July 1994

I looked at this month's young adult event calendar and came across an interesting prayer about being a single person. The prayer, "A Time to Be Single," was a St. Anthony's prayer about our time being single.

CHAPTER 13

A SINGULARLY MOVING PRAYER

"A Time to Be Single" (A Prayer)

Everyone longs to give themselves completely to someone, to have a deep soul relationship with another, to be loved thoroughly and exclusively. But to a Christian God says, "No, not until you are satisfied with being loved by me alone and have an intensely personal, unique relationship with me alone. I love you my child and until you discover that only in me is your satisfaction, you will not be capable of the perfect human relationship that I have planned for you. I want you to stop planning, stop wanting and allow me to bring it to you. Just keep watching me, expecting the greatest things, keep experiencing that satisfaction, knowing that I am, keep learning and listening to the things I tell you. You must wait. Don't be anxious. Don't worry! Don't look around at the things others have gotten or that I have given them. Don't look at the things you want. Just keep looking to me or you will miss what I want to show you. And then when you are ready, I will surprise you with a love far more wonderful than any you would ever dream of. You'll see. Until you are ready, and even this minute I am working to have both of you ready at the same time. Until you are both satisfied with me and the life I have prepared for you, you won't be able to experience the love that exemplifies your relationship with me and is thus perfect love. And dear one, I want you to have this most wonderful love. I want you to see in the flesh a picture of your relationship with me and to enjoy the everlasting union of beauty and love. I am God. Believe and be satisfied."

This prayer really spoke to me about the issues I had been dealing with in my life. From the outside looking in, I had seen how others dated and later got married. Yes, I was focusing a lot on myself in this situation.

God, I have been waiting for so long to find that special someone. Where is she? I feel like I have been stuck in this same situation for so long! God, why are taking so long to bring that person into my life! It is so hard to deal with this loneliness.

I had to admit that I did not have much of a faith life. I really did not have a strong relationship with God. But, God said I needed to focus on Him. *OK, God, but bring her to me soon!*

CHAPTER 14
FLYING SOLO

August 1994

It was that time again to start a new school year in the RE program. I was expecting the call, as preparations were being made to find and recruit an adequate number of RE teachers to teach students in the class room.

* * *

What Comes to Mind

I received that call from the assistant RE director. "Mike," she said, "I wanted to call you to see if you would be interested in teaching again this year. Lisa has decided to go back to school. Can you lead a class this year?"

To be honest, I did not expect to be asked that question. I assumed that I would just be helping out again.

But I replied, "Yes, I will do it."

* * *

She thanked me for offering to volunteer again this year. She also mentioned that she would notify me about the upcoming RE teacher workshops next month. I hung up the phone and sat down in my chair. I spent a few minutes in silence thinking about what just happened.

I said yes. *Am I really ready to lead a class all by myself?* I had immediately said yes. There must be some reason why I wanted to do it. But why?

* * *

However, I later found out that the RE staff was not able to find an assistant for me. I was going to be on my own. *Don't panic.* We were still using the same lesson plans from last year. I just thought about what Lisa lectured to the kids last year.

But I am not a teacher! So what am I going to do? Then a past memory came to mind.

1971: Bored to Tears

"Mike," my teacher said to me, "what are you doing?"

I was in my uncomfortable chair, looking down at my desk, doodling on a piece of paper with a pen.

"Mike, put your pen down and look at me," she replied.

I looked up at her and said, "Nothing."

I was in my second-grade Sunday school class. That morning we were learning stuff about Jesus. The teacher was just talking on and on. Blah, blah, blah… It never stopped. *I am so bored.*

The memory passed and I returned to the present. I did not want to bore my students like my teacher bored me in class. I was going to ask my students questions and talk about my experiences. I figured that the kids got enough lecturing in regular school. I wanted to try to make this RE class fun for them.

Finding That Sweet Spot

It was that time again to start another year of teaching the RE class. In my preparation for class, I was able to find some creative ways to present my lesson plans in class. I used games, trivia, and other fun exercises. And, in turn, the students felt comfortable participating and sharing their thoughts. It seemed like the students were having fun in class.

As the months passed, preparing for my class had felt less like work, and more as a labor of love. In teaching the class, I was also learning and sharing my faith. It just felt right for me to do it. Not sure what it was, but I wanted to keep doing it. At least I felt something was going right in my life. But not everything.

CHAPTER 15
GETTING INTO THE SPIRIT OF THINGS

1997

Despite some difficulties, I was slowly establishing my accounting career. In addition to teaching RE, I found myself wanting to learn more about my faith. I discovered Christian authors, went to conferences, and attended classes and lectures in order to obtain an RE teacher certification. It then dawned on me that I was becoming a different person. My faith had become important to me.

Over the years in the singles group, I continued to make new friends and friendships, but nothing really developed into a dating relationship. Nothing had really changed for me in that aspect of my life. Ironically, up until now, I had never even considered the idea of attending home Mass or any spiritual function in my singles group. I am not exactly sure why. It never even crossed my mind. But, now I felt it was time for me to do this. It was time to get into the spirit of things, to be with others who also have their faith.

CHAPTER 16
A DANCE ENCOUNTER WITH HER

1997

I was planning on attending a young adult event for singles sponsored by the diocese. The event, beginning with Mass and concluding with a dinner and dance, was created in recognition of the various young adult groups throughout the city. I was looking forward to seeing friends and new faces from other groups. I carpooled with my friends and we sat together in church.

* * *

As we left the church, we proceeded into the nearby gym, where tables covered half of the gym floor. The other half of the gym was cleared for dancing, following the dinner. We found a table and sat down, seeing all the other singles coming into the gym. Off to the side, the kitchen staff was preparing the meal to be served to us shortly.

In the meantime, some of the attendees remained seated at their tables. There were some newcomers from our group, whom I hadn't seen before. A petite young woman sat at the end our long table. Among the newcomers, she briefly caught my attention. She was beautiful. I had never seen her before. Others were gathering in the empty part of the gym, socializing with each other. I decided to get up and join them and introduce myself. I was curious to see which groups and parishes were represented here at this event.

As we were eating our spaghetti dinner, still more singles showed up, primarily interested in dancing. As dinner was winding down, preparations were being made for the dance. The DJ was setting up his equipment. Tables were being set up and stocked with drinks and refreshments. In the meantime, the young adults were again gathering together and socializing.

The music was starting and many people were heading to the dance floor. Some of us, who were talking to each other, started to dance. Others returned to their tables. That young woman, who briefly caught my attention, joined us on the dance floor. We all casually danced together in a large group. I looked at her name tag. I was quite surprised to learn that she and I attended the same church. Yet, I had never seen her until now. We briefly introduced ourselves and continued to dance. She was so beautiful. I tried not to stare at her. However, as the music played on, she noticed my brief side glances toward her throughout the music. Later on during the dance, I wanted to see if she would like to dance with me. However, I couldn't find the courage to ask her. I missed the chance to have that dance with her.

CHAPTER 17
A SAFARI SO GOOD

A field trip to the nearby botanical gardens in Galveston was scheduled the next Saturday morning. I was planning on attending the event. We were to meet at a parking lot to carpool. We were fortunate in that our singles group was getting larger in recent months. Since I had always remembered being warmly welcomed into the group, it was always nice to reciprocate and welcome other newcomers. At a given time, you would never know how many could show up at a given event.

* * *

I arrived at our scheduled meeting place and I saw her again. She was leaning against a car. I got out of my car and walked toward her. I was surprised and pleasantly so. I was definitely looking forward to this trip. This was my opportunity to talk to her and get to know a little more about her. She had a wonderful smile.

"Hello," I said, "I am Mike."

She introduced herself to me. I also found out that she too had never been to the botanical gardens. Before we could get further into our conversation, other people showed up in the parking lot. We were scheduled to leave at 10:00 am. We decided to wait a few more minutes before leaving.

Four other people showed up. Three friends that I had already known and a newcomer to the group. It was decided that we would take two cars. She offered to drive some of us in her car. I not surprisingly and gladly decided to sit in the front seat next to her. This was going to be a great opportunity to get to know a little more about her. In the hour it took driving to the gardens, I really enjoyed talking with her.

Again, I found myself, every now and then, making sideway glances toward her, as she was looking ahead driving.

* * *

We finally arrived and entered the botanical garden facilities. As we took in the sights, I wanted to further know about her. Again, she looked so beautiful. We walked and talked, and I treasured every moment of this experience just being with her.

* * *

We decided to stop at a restaurant for lunch in Galveston before we headed home. We enjoyed talking about our experiences at the gardens. Upon finishing our meal, I saw that our waiter brought a small piece of cake for her. I soon learned that today was her birthday. Evidently, her friend told the waiter it was her birthday. What a wonderful way to end this day, celebrating her birthday. It was like I was meant to be with her on this special day.

CHAPTER 18
THERE IS NO PLACE LIKE A SPIRITUAL HOME

One evening I was planning on attending Spiritual Growth. This was going to be my first time going to an event like this in our group. I wondered why I never considered it before. Actually, the place wasn't too far from where I lived. I found the apartment complex with no problem. As I was heading to the apartment number, I noticed some of my friends and others were heading in the same direction. At least, I found the right place. We found the apartment and someone knocked on the door. The door opened and there she was again.

She said, "I am glad you all can make it tonight. Come on in. We're going to get started pretty soon."

I immediately looked at her and thought to myself, "Hmm…it happened again…" It really got me thinking.

I smiled and said, "I am glad I'm here."

The ten of us were chatting with each other. She, trying to get our attention, said, "Welcome. We have refreshments in the kitchen and some desserts on the table for later. Let's get started."

We concluded our spiritual gathering, consisting of Scripture study, personal sharing, exercises, and games. We ended with prayers and later gathered together in the kitchen to eat, drink, and talk. This was a very enjoyable experience for me. I wanted to do it again. I never had felt more right at home.

As the months continued, I regularly attended Spiritual Growth. I immediately saw that her faith and the Spiritual Growth group were very important to her. Out of friendship, I was happy to share my experiences, insights, and resources with the group. I belonged there. It felt the same as when I was teaching my high school students at church. Whether with my peers or high school kids, it made no difference. I wasn't sure why, but it made me feel right at home.

CHAPTER 19
BLURRED VISION

I really wanted to contribute as a friend in any way I could at Spiritual Growth. I felt it was important for me that I do this. Then I realized that I was beginning to have feelings for her. These feelings were gradually becoming stronger over the months. I wasn't sure if she was aware of this. I tried to keep these feelings to myself. But I wondered if she could have feelings for me. I was seeing her in a different light.

She Was Unavailable at This Moment

I was trying to find the courage to ask her if she was interested in going out with me. I wasn't ready to ask her in person. Doing this over the phone seemed less scary for me.

"Hi," I said, "this is Mike. I was wondering if you would be interested in going out with me." There was silence.

Then she said, "You know, I'm flattered that you would ask me. But I have to say no." She left it at, without further explanation. More silence.

I replied, "OK. Well, you can't blame a guy for trying. See you around." I hung up the phone. I received her message.

Spiritual Ties That Bind

At least I knew where I stood with her. Yes, I was disappointed, but I had to respect her wishes. I continued attending Spiritual Growth, as I saw no reason that I should stop going. I just needed to keep a respectful distance from her. There were times when attendance dwindled. I could see that she was disappointed about this. I wanted to utilize my experience and resources to generate further interest in people showing up at Spiritual Growth. I still cared for her as a friend.

* * *

During this time a strange thing was happening with me. My feelings for her were increasing and intensifying. *Why is this happening to me? I am not pursuing her in a dating relationship.* She made that very clear for me. I just couldn't shake the feelings. I kept asking and praying. *Why can't I get rid of these feelings?* I received no answer or clue to this. *Why God, why can't I get rid of these feelings!* I was in an emotional bind.

CHAPTER 20
HER FACE THAT LAUNCHED 1000 TEARS

August 1998

It was that time again to celebrate her birthday. This year we celebrated her birthday party at a restaurant. Unlike last year's small birthday celebration, a large number of friends showed up. I attended the event, keeping a respectful distance from her. After our meal we celebrated her birthday with cake. When we concluded the celebration, several of us came and hugged her to wish her happy birthday. I was included among these people. I was still her friend, so I thought it would be OK if I could give her a friendly hug before leaving. After all, we were just in a restaurant.

My Emotional Dam Bursts

I looked into her eyes. I gave her a friendly hug. I then headed out the restaurant. As I was heading back home, I realized that something was happening to me. My feelings intensified, like a dam about to burst. I couldn't hold them in. For so long, I had been trying to hold and contain these feelings. But the feelings rushed up to the surface, releasing a deluge of emotions. I was crying, but I didn't understand it. *What is going on?* Then it dawned on me. These were tears of joy! I was able to experience these feelings for the first time in my life!

For the next two weeks, I was an emotional wreck. I would find myself uncontrollably tearing up when I least expected it. I finally realized that I had fallen in love with her. I was trying to figure this out. It was such a profound emotional experience, that I cried as a result of it. But the reality had immediately set in. She, although emotionally close to me, was still far away. Again, I was on the outside looking in.

Butterflies Are Free!

What I am going to do now? I have to tell her about this. How is she going to react to this? The only time that I would see her was when I went to Spiritual Growth. So I needed to talk to her in private, before the others came. I decided to go to her place twenty minutes early.

I knocked on her door. As she opened the door, I looked into her eyes. It seemed as if time stood still for a very brief moment. It was as if I was tethered to her eyes. Then something else suddenly happened to me.

I immediately thought to myself, "Wait, what was that?" I felt something in my stomach. It was hard to explain. I felt a queasy, warm, and stinging sensation in my gut. *Are those butterflies? I haven't experienced this since I was very young.* Butterflies are free. I didn't see that coming!

I finally was able to get out of my stupor and get back into the present moment. I told her that I had fallen in love with her! She immediately let me in. She clearly was upset and disturbed about what I had just told her.

However, still understanding, she sat down and said, "What can I do to help?"

How did I get myself in this situation? I have fallen in love with someone who is unavailable to me! I was almost at the point of having to apologize for putting her in this situation. *What is going on with my life!* I told her that I would need to continue to maintain a discrete distance from her. By the time we finished our conversation, the others were arriving for Spiritual Growth.

Caught in an Emotional Net

In the months that followed, I continued going to Spiritual Growth. *After all, I am an RE teacher. This is what I do.* Other than the group, I was not really involved in her life. I was trying to get on with my life. On the small chance that we would show up at a given event, I would continue to stay clear from her. I could not get rid of these feelings. I begged and pleaded to God to help me. *How am I supposed to get on with my life?* Unlike those butterflies, I was caught in this emotional net.

CHAPTER 21
EASY AS π

Getting Benched by My Spiritual Coach

I need help. What am I supposed to do? I can't get rid of these feelings!

I decided to meet with my pastor for some advice on how to handle this situation. After explaining my predicament and my reasons for attending Spiritual Growth, the priest offered me some advice. However, I knew it was going to be very difficult for me to take his advice. After some thought, I did what he suggested. I stopped going to Spiritual Growth. I only attended the monthly home Mass and potluck dinner events.

Shortly thereafter, something unexpected happened to me. My feelings for her actually intensified! Why did this happen? I was trying to get rid of my feelings! I thought about it for a while. Did I do something to cause this to happen? Although I could never have been a part in her life, she still had become important to me.

Is that why my feelings have increased? I guess I really do love her! Wait a minute! I am trying to get rid of these feelings! How do I figure out this %#*=+<>π♥ equation?

Her Poker Face

Several months later another curious thing happened while I was going to 7:30 am Sunday Mass. Just as I was heading into the church, I saw her coming out of the gathering center next door. Since she normally attended the 10:30 am Mass, I usually did not see her on Sundays. I stopped, waved, and said hello, very reluctant about approaching her. It was just too emotionally difficult for me to be close to her. She saw me. Then her face lit up with a big smile. I was taken aback, not sure how to react to this. It really got me thinking. *Could it be possible?* I tried to hide my surprise and then entered the church. *Maybe she does have feelings for me!*

* * *

A week later, a game night was scheduled at a friend's apartment. I arrived early. As I was talking to my friends, I noticed that she later showed up. As she entered inside, she saw me. She approached me and said, "When I saw you Sunday morning… I hope I didn't give you the wrong impression." She left it at that. I thought about what she had just said, and I did not say anything. I really didn't know what to think.

Why did she feel that she had to explain herself? Now what am I supposed to think? Is it, "Methinks the lady doth protest too much?" Or is this another disappointment for me?

At that moment, I needed to walk away and talk to someone else. I laid my cards on the table, but was she holding all the cards?

CHAPTER 22
TO MY SURPRISE!

A Birthday Surprise

It was again time to celebrate her birthday at another restaurant. I made the decision to attend the event. Just like last year, many friends came. As I sat down, I noticed that she hadn't shown up yet. Perhaps she was running late. Later she arrived, but she wasn't alone. She was with some other guy, whom I had never seen before. She was holding his hand! This image was permanently etched in my mind. I was beginning to get upset. I tried not to show it. But I couldn't just leave. I needed to compose myself to get through it. I wanted to get out of there. But it seemed like the event lasted forever.

It finally ended. I said my goodbyes to my friends seated next to me. But I couldn't face her. I just couldn't do it. I immediately headed out to my car, upset. *What am I supposed to do now? I have to do something!*

I remembered that there was a church nearby, with a twenty-four hour Eucharistic chapel. Perhaps I wasn't in the best state of mind to drive, but somehow I made it to the chapel. Again, I was on the outside looking in.

I entered the circular-shaped window chapel. No one else was there at that time of the night. Three rows of kneelers surrounded the center of the chapel. I went to the first row and knelt down. I was still very much upset, almost to the point of crying. It was a good thing that no one else was around to see me make a spectacle of myself. It was just Jesus and me.

I immediately cried out, "Why did it have to be this way? I finally found someone important to me. But she can't be part of my life! I have been waiting all my life to have these feelings. It was just so hard seeing her with that other guy."

I tried to settle down, be still and quiet, and gather my thoughts. I cried out, "Lord, I just don't understand it. I thought that she was going to be the one for me!"

I finally was able to calm down a little, but I still was having a hard time accepting this situation. *What do I do now? How am I supposed to get on with my life?* I really did not have anything more to say at that moment, I decided to head on home. *This just can't be happening to me! It just doesn't make sense. This has to be a dream!*

CHAPTER 23
FASTEN YOUR SEAT BELTS

2008: I Have Just Fallen in Love and I Can't Get Up!

In the years ahead, some things changed in my life and some things stayed the same. I finally was starting to establish my career. However, I never was able to get rid of those feelings. So I was never able to consider the idea of finding someone else. As the years passed, she and I lived our separate lives.

She eventually married that guy. As for me, I was stuck in an emotional rabbit hole, and I never was able to get out of it.

The Roller-Coaster Ride Continues

It was as if I was still riding the roller coaster, experiencing the twists and turns of life. I traveled to the heights of career success and the depths of loneliness. Yet, I found myself stranded on this track, caught in my own emotional breaking system. And I didn't see that coming!

2012: Back to the Future

I introduced myself to my class. "Welcome. I am going to be your teacher this year. I am looking forward to having you all in my class. My name is Mike. I have been teaching this class since 1993. Let's get started…"

CHAPTER 23
"I'LL TAKE VOCATIONS FOR $200, ALEX…"

2008: And Now for the Rest of the Story

Yes, I have been an RE teacher and have been doing this for quite a while. Yet, I really never thought about why. That thought had never really crossed my mind, until now. I remembered when Dave had first asked me that question. I remembered all the struggles and adversity. I remembered wanting to escape from them. OK, that explains why I decided to do this in the first place. But this is just the beginning of the story.

In my years of teaching, I have seen many other volunteer teachers and assistants come and go. I have seen a few remain, but more leave. "I tried, but it's just not for me," is usually the common response. However, it's not my place to make any value judgements for their reasons or motivation. Let's be honest, teaching teenagers in an RE class could be a very difficult challenge for some people.

I would wager that the majority of these persons were already pursuing their own vocations in their lives. Perhaps they were already focused on their own vocations as a spouse, father, mother, son, daughter, or their career, or school. And they just didn't have the time to do something else. That's certainly understandable. On the other hand, singles may have greater freedom, availability, or time to serve others.

Yet, on the other hand, I have remained single. Why? Possibly it could be determined by a person's talents, skills, and abilities. This could very well true. However, to be honest, I really didn't fully know what I was getting myself into when I first started as an RE teacher. I didn't know I had these abilities in the first place. But more importantly, because of my situation, I had the freedom and time to pursue this endeavor.

Looking back, I remembered I had thrust myself into teaching to escape from my difficulties. As a result, I tapped into something which later resulted in a vocation or calling. When or how this call had happened, I really cannot say. What is more important is that I found this calling. Although I never really understood, it just felt right for me for me to do this.

Receiving a Good WI-FI (Wireless Fidelity) Connection From God

What is a lay vocation? This is the calling or destiny we have in this life and hereafter.

It is interesting to note that, through these struggles, I found my other calling (vocation) as an accountant. These vocations, although different, both have allowed me to utilize my gifts and talents in my life. It took me quite a while to figure out that I was called to be an accountant. Not only do I enjoy accounting, I am good at it. In other words, I was hardwired to be an accountant.

Although an old religious education book may be old, it still provides timeless wisdom about our relationship with God. One old book states, "What must we do to gain the happiness of heaven?" In other words, "Why did God make you?" In its simplicity, we must know, love, and serve God in this world. In a nutshell, we are hardwired to serve God. It is only when we find this connection that we are happiest in our lives.

So I understand what it means to struggle as a single person. It is only natural to dwell on our situation when experiencing loneliness and lack of purpose in our life. For all those who are questioning why they are still single: focus on God and less on yourself and perhaps you may receive a better WI-FI connection.

That Sounds Greek to Me

What does catechesis mean? This term comes from the Greek *katechizien*, which means to teach orally. The Greek *kata* means thoroughly or down. The Greek *echein* means to sound thoroughly. Essentially, catechesis means to send out and transmit the faith. An RE teacher shares one's faith and teaches by questions and answers.

This concludes our Greek exegesis exercise, now we will return to my regularly scheduled story. So again why did I teach high school kids for so long? It is because I found a place where God was calling me to be in my life. It's sometimes hard to explain, but it just feels right for me.

Unwrapping That Gift

Whether they are teenagers or young adults, I realized I found a place sharing my faith and serving others. It really doesn't matter whom I am talking with. To be honest, my situation is not really different from others. A husband and wife become a gift to each other, as they care for each other. A mother becomes a gift of herself, as she takes care of her sick child. A wife becomes a gift of herself, when she cares for her husband suffering from dementia. A priest becomes a gift of himself as a spiritual father to his congregation. A religious nun becomes a gift of herself to others in the service of her order.

What does Luke's Gospel say about this? Luke 17:33 states, "Whoever seeks to preserve his life will lose it, but whoever loses it will save it." The Scripture passage clearly shows how one can find oneself.

CHAPTER 25
GETTING ON BOARD GOD'S PROVIDENCE EXPRESS

How did I feel about leaving Spiritual Growth? This was a very difficult decision for me to make in a complicated situation. I didn't know what to do at the time. So, I took the advice of one of God's agents and made other travel plans away from Spiritual Growth. I had always wondered why I decided to go to Spiritual Growth at a certain point in time. I had been an RE teacher for several years, yet I never felt the desire to attend Spiritual Growth. Why? Perhaps, I wasn't ready. Another young adult was the Spiritual Growth leader at the time. Little did I know that she, whom I would later encounter, had not yet joined our singles group. She was still in Kansas. She, at that time, had not yet moved to Houston to start her new job. Then, she, unbeknownst to me, became the leader of Spiritual Growth. So, God really does play an important part (behind the scenes) in bringing people, although briefly, into others' lives.

CHAPTER 26

GOD, IS THAT WHAT YOU DO?

Leaving Home

I really felt at home at Spiritual Growth, sharing my faith, experiences, and resources with my peers. If you are an RE teacher, you share your faith. It's what you do. I contributed to the group out of friendship toward her. As I had already found her attractive, my feelings toward her naturally increased. Since we are called to share our faith unconditionally, it was difficult to determine if I did this out of friendship or love. When it comes unconditionally, I could see how the lines between friendship and love can be blurred. With that being said, it was difficult to tell when friendship ended and love began. This was the path I had followed. I had found a spiritual home, but it was difficult for me to leave. Yet, I had to make this decision. And, it was the right decision at the time.

I made the very difficult decision to leave Spiritual Growth. Yet, why did my feelings suddenly increase? I really did not expect that to happen. As a practical matter, I thought these feelings would subside. I just didn't understand this. Here I was, caught in the greatest irony of all. I had been waiting all my life looking for someone important to me. I finally found that person, but she was not able to become part of my life. Then, I had to let her go, so I could get on with my life.

God. You already know about all the loneliness in my life. You already know how I felt about never even having a girlfriend.

I really thought I finally found her this time, that she was the one for me. We both found our faith. After all I had gone through in my life, I thought this time He would make it simple for me. As time went on, her welfare had become more important to me. I later realized that I had often made her feel uncomfortable at times in the past. So was that why I had let her go? Did I place her welfare above my own? Is that why my feelings increased?

But I was trying to get rid of these feelings! God, you really pulled a good joke on me. God, is this what you do?

CHAPTER 27
A SINGLE-MINDED IDEA

2008

I continued on with my life being "stuck" with these feelings for her. This situation enabled me to really think about what it means to be a single person. I wanted to learn about how other singles cope with this. I just wanted to try to make sense of what I was going through in my life. I learned that I was not alone. In a way, I was not much different from others who were still looking for that special someone. I was starting to better understand my singleness.

Since having these feelings, how can I consider the possibility of dating again? How would it be fair to the other person? However, it became a moot point, since no one else ever showed up.

As I look back, I found my vocation in part because of my struggles as a single person. Somehow, I had this sense that I would have this RE teacher vocation for the rest of my life. I saw myself as an RE teacher and accountant, but still single. But as I later continued to understand what singleness means, I sensed a change. I was not exactly sure what it was. I sensed that no one would be coming to me. Perhaps marriage was not meant to be for me.

I noticed my feelings were finally beginning to subside. But why now? For so many years, I had prayed that I could get rid of these feelings, so that I could get on with my life. But God never answered my prayers. It was as if God was holding my feelings hostage, not letting me go. Here is an interesting thought. Maybe, I was the one who was changing. The ideas of dating and even marriage were becoming less important to me.

To be honest, I really never thought about how much God plays a role in guiding one's path in life. But I have come to think about this more lately. What was God doing behind the scenes? He was shaping and molding me to be the person He wants me to be. I realized that there could be no other answer. God had answered my prayers in the way He saw fit. God had a single-minded purpose in giving me a lay single vocation.

Unanswered Prayer Poem

When prayers aren't answered
Quickly or right away,
Just ask the Lord to reveal to you,
The reason for His delay.

If the answer for that request
Just seems to take too long
Just lift up your hands
And praise Him
With a glorious new song.

Just wait on the Lord
And try to be still
'Cause your request may not be
In God's will.

If that is the case
Just praise Him again
He won't steer you wrong
'Cause He's your friend.

Maybe you'll learn patience,
A little trust too.
Or maybe your motives
You'll need to review.

Ask Him for an answer
The way He sees fit.
But don't you lose hope
And don't you quit.

The answer can be revealed
In a miraculous way.
So be prepared to listen
To what He has to say.

The answer will bring Him
Honor and glory.
And then you'll be able to tell
Your story.

Minister to those
Who did lose hope.
Who were looking for answers
On how to cope.

CHAPTER 28
PROCEED WITH CAUTION:
DETOURS, OBSTACLES (AND IRONIES) AHEAD

The Roller-Coaster Ride Starts Again

OK. I have a lay single vocation. What do I do now?
With this lay single vocation, God has again released the
emotional brakes for another ride on this roller coaster. He

has set me on another path to my destination. I faced many speed bumps, obstacles, and stumbling blocks on the way here. However, Eternal God, outside of time, already knew my path. Perhaps, by looking from where I came from, I can learn how I arrived here today.

God: The Providential Personal Trainer

Whether by my own choices and/or by God's providence, I encountered many difficulties and obstacles in sports, relationships, and career. Although I tried to do my best, I always seemed to struggle in these efforts. For some reason, it had never come easy to me. Perhaps, God was already shaping and molding me to face the obstacles and difficulties that would later come. As I was just living my life, I seemed to face stumbling blocks seen and unseen.

I thought that I had held some promise as a Little League baseball player. I was proud of my abilities, with so much potential. Yet, years later, I was faced with the humbling reality of the limitations of my physical abilities and my little brother surpassing me in two sports. God was preparing me to be able to face difficulties and challenges. God was preparing me to face new paths.

OK. So baseball is not my sport. I can deal with that. But basketball was my game. After all, I was on several championship teams. I was the big man on my team. But something else happened. I faced an unseen stumbling block, I stopped growing. Come high school, I couldn't compete even as a small guard. This forced me to end my basketball career. Again, God was saying: "Mike, I have other plans for you." Like a spiritual coach, God was training me to become the person I am today.

God: The Cosmic Career Counselor

I really thought I had made the right career choice to pursue pharmacy. I realized that this was going to be a difficult and challenging career path. I knew I could accomplish it. After all, I did graduate from high school with *cum laude* honors. As I pursued these studies, I found myself struggling with more and more classes. Despite the struggles, I really did not consider the idea of changing my major. I did not want to start over again. The greatest irony of all was that I later had to start over again to obtain my accounting degree.

Of course, I did not know that would happen to me, but God obviously already knew. So this begs the question of what part God could have played in this drama. Looking back, I would say that God may have placed obstacles before me in my pursuit of pharmacy. For the life of me, I just couldn't understand why I struggled so much during this time. Perhaps, in His Providence, God permitted me to experience these struggles, allowing me to find another path, a better path for me. Although it took a while, God eventually guided and helped me to find the right career path. God, the highest school career counselor of them all, already knew that I needed a career change.

God: The Majestic Matchmaker

I just never could understand why I never had a girlfriend all throughout my life. This became a great irony in my life. I was preoccupied with something which I never could have. While growing up, I really did not see myself any different from friends and peers. Of course, this really did not help my self-confidence or self-esteem. Nobody wanted to be with me. I did not have the faith life to even consider the possibility of becoming a priest. So that was never in the cards of the life that I had been dealt.

49

Why did I never have a girlfriend? Obviously, I didn't know back then. Don't get me wrong. I really felt that I had lost out, never having that experience in my life. So many times, I felt jealous and envious of those who did. My brother and sister are both married now and have children. I was always happy for them, but still it was hard for me to accept that there was no one there for me. But what could I have done? It was just that no one could see me in that way. I felt like that outsider looking in.

Then I thought that I finally found that special person in my life. I had found someone important to me. However, she couldn't be a part of my life. Yet I wonder, why did God allow this? I guess I will never know for sure. Perhaps, He allowed me to have a "taste" of what it means to have someone important to me. Then these feelings eventually subsided.

But I think I may know now. God had other plans for me. Looking back, it is as if God was preparing me for my single vocation. God would be using my single state to better serve Him. I was just viewing my life from my own perspective, not understanding or making sense of this path. Now, by focusing on God, I was beginning to see the bigger picture. God was opening my eyes to allow me to see a bigger perspective on why I have been single. It is as if God was giving me a peek from His perspective.

CHAPTER 29
WHAT IS A SINGLE PERSON TO DO?

Fear of Being Alone

I experienced this loneliness for most of my life. It had been always easy for me to identify this fear: no one was ever interested in me. This fear and loneliness were always on my mind. I spent more time alone, dwelling on my situation. I really didn't bring God into the equation. After all, I was just a kid. It was years later that I was given an opportunity to teach high school kids. At that time, I just wanted to do something to shift the focus away from what I had been experiencing in my life. Because of this, I was able find my vocation.

Focusing on God

In my studies in what it means to be a single person, I have learned some valuable insights. Instead of dwelling on my own situation, I should have focused more attention on God. Instead, I tried to deal with this all on my own. God wants us to be honest with Him and with our feelings. God can take it. Tell Him what's on your mind. You won't hurt God's feelings. By giving your problem to God, it becomes His problem.

Complete as One

For so long, I have always felt that I was lacking or incomplete as a single person. I had never felt the calling to be a priest. So, that was never in the cards. With that in mind, I thought marriage was going to be the path for me. So, I felt incomplete. Besides, what else was there for me? Marriage was becoming the end all and be all thing for me.

As I was learning what it means to be a single person, the Holy Spirit was opening my eyes, allowing me to see the bigger picture about marriage. I was discovering that marriage is only a temporary, earthly institution. I was beginning to see that God seeks to encounter us, whether we are single or married. I was finding out that being single is not an excuse for waiting for that person or waiting for life to happen.

Yet, if it weren't for these struggles, I never would have found my vocation. I never realized how much my vocation has meant to me. It has allowed me to make sense of my struggles and has allowed me to find some purpose and meaning in my life. God has helped me to feel complete as a single person.

CHAPTER 30
IDOL THOUGHTS ABOUT
MARRIAGE AND SINGLENESS

Taking the Blinders Off

Like many of my peers, I held some preconceived notions about marriage. I have always believed that things happen for a reason. Yet, I could never understand why no one was ever interested in me. Maybe it was just that I hadn't found that person yet. How else could I have explained my situation? Then she comes into my life. Then I later find out we are both spiritual-growth leaders in our singles group. So, she must be the one for me. I finally found her.

I did not want to remain single for so long in my life. I told God I was tired of going through this. *God, at least take away this desire to be married.* But God didn't answer my prayers. Even after having feelings for someone who could never be a part of my life, I asked God to take these feelings away, so I could get on with my life. But again God didn't answer my prayers. *So, God, why are you leaving me in this limbo?* Then He finally answered my prayers. God took away the desire for marriage and granted me the gift of singleness.

CHAPTER 31
LOOKING OUT FROM GOD'S CASTLE

As I was traveling down this complicated path, I was seeing things in my life from a narrow perspective. God sees the big picture, a bigger perspective. While I was still learning what it means to be single, God already knew my path. I am now seeing, that from God's wider perspective, singleness has a purpose with multiple blessings and great value in the kingdom of heaven. His Son Jesus and the Apostle Paul are prime examples. With the help of the Holy Spirit, I am now seeing my life through a wider lens, a wider perspective. What I thought were struggles have now became blessings in disguise. It was as if God had already known that I would make a greater difference in other peoples' lives as a single person.

God says that true joy is found in serving others. So, it is not surprising that God has always taught us to help others. You do not need to take my word for it. Whether we serve the homeless at soup kitchens or adopt a needy family at Christmas, we feel good about making a small difference in others' lives. I also have been very fortunate to the have opportunity to catechize teenagers and young adults over the years. I really did not fully appreciate that when I was teaching and sharing my faith with others, I was actually serving others.

Getting Over Myself

For so long, I didn't understand why I experienced so many struggles in my life. At the time, I focused upon myself, and I felt lost and adrift. Then something happened along the way. Later, by focusing on others, I found myself with a purpose and a vocation.

I also have learned that God will bless singles with more children than being married. At first glance, this may sound like nonsense. But, once you really think about it, it does make sense. A priest is a spiritual father to his congregation. The nun is a spiritual mother to her students. I myself, was given the opportunity to hopefully plant a few seeds of faith to the many ("my") high school kids over the years. God allowed me the opportunity to reach many more kids than if I had kids of my own. So God did really send more kids to me.

We Are Prophets of a Future Not Our Own
~ Archbishop Oscar Romero

It helps, now and then, to step back and take the long view.
The Kingdom is not only beyond our efforts,
It is beyond our vision.
We accomplish in our lifetime only a tiny fraction of
the magnificent enterprise that is God's work.
We plant seeds already planted, know that
they hold future promise.
We cannot do everything
and there is a sense of liberation in realizing that.
This enables us to do something,
and do it very well.
It may be incomplete, but it is a beginning,
a step along the way,
an opportunity for God's grace to enter and do the rest.
We may never see the end results,
but that is the difference between the master builders,
and the worker.
We are workers, not master builders,
ministers, not messiahs.
We are prophets of a future not our own.

CHAPTER 32
BETTER BLESSINGS AND GIFTS

I have learned that single people, who follow the Lord, will receive the promise of better blessings and gifts. Isaiah 56:4-5 states that a monument and name, better than sons and daughters, is given to those who follow Him. This monument serves to give an everlasting name to those who do not have physical offspring.

So here I am. How did I get here? I was just living my life, riding that roller coaster. Moving through those twists and turns, peaks and drops. I had a bumpy ride. I was moving forward, but with no purpose or direction. Then I found myself stuck, unable to move ahead. God came and released me from my emotional restraints and lead me to my destination. God, who already knew my path, allowed me to find Him and bring me back home. Now I have a single lay vocation. And I really didn't see that coming!

CHAPTER 33
RELATIONSHIPS: A MATCH MADE IN HEAVEN

Making Early Vocation Plans

When I was growing up, I did not have the spiritual faith or sense to even consider the priesthood. It just wasn't on my "radar." So now, my path continues to be "in the trenches" and engaged in the world. However, I would encourage you moms and dads to be open to the possibility that your child might seek that different path. For young boys, this could be the priesthood or being a brother in a religious community. For young girls, this could be being a nun or the consecrated life. With your prayers, perhaps, they may find their rewarding travel destination in life.

I Am in a Relationship Now (So to Speak)

For so many years I had experienced cluelessness, worry, anxiety, and grief when it came to dating relationships. It just wasn't happening for me. Now realizing that this wasn't God's path for me, I feel a huge weight has been lifted off my shoulders! This has given me a sense of peace. How ironic it is that instead of seeing an attractive woman as a potential date or girlfriend material, I have a much greater appreciation and respect for her as a single person.

CHAPTER 34
WHAT DOES THE OLD TESTAMENT SAY ABOUT SINGLENESS?

"Be fertile and multiply; fill the earth and subdue it" (Genesis 1:28).

This was basically God's commandment to increase the family of God into the future. Marriage and procreation were divinely ordained and encouraged. These practices were seen as normal and expected for all created life. The head of the family did not have an expectation of a personal afterlife. The father's name and legacy were in a sense immortalized through his descendants. Rather, they saw themselves living on through their children, especially their male descendants.

"The Lord God said, 'It is not good for the man to be alone. I will make a suitable partner for him'" (Genesis 2:18).

Singleness was not given a place of honor in the Old Testament. Singleness was not discussed. To be single was almost like not having life after death. The children's fate was ordinarily determined by arranged marriages. The daughter was essentially considered as property of the family. A groom's family typically purchased a dowry for the bride. This contract allowed the father to give the bride away in the marriage tradition. Today, the father's giving away the bride symbolizes his blessing of the marriage.

"Then God remembered Rachel, He heard her prayer and made her fruitful. She conceived and bore a son and she said, 'God has removed my disgrace'" (Genesis 30:22-23).

"Then Jephthah said to her father, 'Let me have this favor. Spare me for two months, that I may go off down the mountains to mourn my virginity with my companions'" (Judges 11:37).

A woman also played a very important role as mother. It was culturally expected and desirable that a woman have children to help perpetuate her husband's name through history. For those women unable to assume this role, it was considered shameful and disgraceful to be unmarried and without a child. This went against the cultural norms of marriage and procreation.

God, the Eternal Pilot

"Before I formed you in the womb, I knew you, before you were born I dedicated you, a prophet to the nations I appointed you" (Jeremiah 2:5).

God, outside of time, already knew Jeremiah's path. So, too, God has already known my path. He was leading me to my destination. Of course, for a long time in my life, I had no clue where my path was leading me. It was only after bringing God into my life that I was able to figure out my path.

"This message came to me from the Lord: 'Do not marry any woman; you shall not have sons or daughters in this place'" (Jeremiah 16:1-2).

Jeremiah was supposed to be a priest. However, God had other plans for Jeremiah. God wanted Jeremiah to remain single. But even Jeremiah argued with God about this. Jeremiah was to be spared witnessing the terrible suffering of a wife and children. Jeremiah's job was to warn the people that the time of curses had come.

God Singled Me Out

Normally, I wouldn't have given this passage any thought. First of all, I was never aware of this passage. Besides, what did this have to do with me? Jeremiah was destined to become a prophet. Unlike Jeremiah, I really didn't have a clue where I was going in my life. At least, I knew I was not going to be a priest. But I was finding myself remaining single and alone throughout my life. I constantly wondered why no one had ever become interested in me. To be honest, this certainly didn't help my confidence and self-esteem.

Now, as I look back at my life, I am seeing this passage in a whole new light. I never really thought about what God's plan was for me. Since I did not have much of a faith, I really did not have the spiritual sense to consider this. But now, I see that this Scripture passage was speaking to my path. God already knew that I would remain single. God would have other plans for me with a lay single vocation. This passage has helped me to make sense of why no else had ever considered me more than as a friend. So, God had other plans for me.

I also never understood why God would allow me to have feelings for someone who could not be available to me. Perhaps, God allowed me to get a "taste" of what it means to have someone important to me. When God took these feelings away, I found myself to be fully receptive to this gift of singleness.

"But the Lord was pleased to crush Him in infirmity. If He give His life as an offering to sin, He shall see His descendants in a long life, and the will of the Lord accomplished through Him" (Isaiah 53:10).

This great saving act will produce many spiritual "children." These children are produced not by physical procreation, but by a covenantal relationship with Jesus. Examples of these children are priests, nuns, religious, and singles.

Calling All Singles

"Raise a glad cry, you barren one who do not bear, break forth in jubilant song, you who were not in labor. For more numerous are the children of the deserted wife than the children of her who has a husband" (Isaiah 54:1). This Scripture really hits home for me. For so long, I had often felt alone, lost, and adrift. This passage has helped me to understand the purpose and destination of the path I had taken. This passage identifies where I am today.

This Scripture passage also speaks to the cultural norm that childbearing and procreation were highly favored. The barren woman often despaired of her situation. The "barren one" represents Jerusalem, who finds herself with innumerable children (the returning exiles). This barren one points to the priest who shepherds his congregation (spiritual children). This barren one points to the nuns and religious who serve many others.

Come Get Your Kids

I can relate to this as I have had the opportunity to encounter and catechize many high school kids and young adults. In my many struggles, I found the opportunity to focus my attention on others.

"For thus says the Lord, 'To the eunuchs who observe my Sabbaths and choose what pleases Me and hold fast to my covenant, I will give, in My house and within my walls, a monument and a name better than sons and daughters; an eternal, imperishable name I will give them'" (Isaiah 56:3-5).

Even as society had often looked down upon eunuchs, God still had a place for those eunuchs who followed Him. God gives great blessing (a great legacy) to those who remain single in Christ. He gives them an extraordinary calling in life. Ordinarily, a man's name and legacy would continue in his children. His sons keep and perpetuate his name in memory.

On the other hand, monuments were often erected to keep the memory of those who could not perpetuate one's name through children. These monuments often lasted longer than a family tree. Generally, these monuments would be more enduring (last longer) than sons and daughters. Absalom, who had no son to perpetuate his name, erected a pillar to commemorate his name in the King's Valley (see 2 Samuel 18:18).

A Monumental Opportunity

Isaiah 54:1 is one of my favorite Scripture passages. This passage has given me great comfort and peace of mind. It has helped me to better make sense and meaning of my path and to understand that there was a purpose behind all of my struggles and difficulties. This passage helps explain why I have found a vocation, which has become important to me.

CHAPTER 35
WHAT DOES THE NEW TESTAMENT SAY ABOUT SINGLENESS?

Singleness is not explicitly stated in the Old Testament. However, the promise of a legacy better than sons and daughters is given to those eunuchs (dry trees) who follow

Him. Singleness is elevated by Jesus and Paul. Jesus and Paul call singleness a gift.

"Indeed, I wish everyone to be as I am, but each has a particular gift from God, one of one kind and one of another" (1 Corinthians 7:7).

Singly Effective

Paul believed that as a single person, one would be the most effective in spreading the Gospel. As a practical matter, I also would agree with this notion. Since I really didn't have a dating life to begin with, I was able to focus much of my time and efforts in my ministry. Unbeknownst to me, I was already using my singleness in becoming the best RE teacher I could be.

"Some are incapable of marriage because they were born so; some, because they were made so by others; some, because they have renounced marriage for the sake of the kingdom. Whoever can accept this ought to accept it" (Matthew 19:12).

Jesus notes that there are three types of eunuchs who are not given to marry. Those born as eunuchs are unable to consummate marriage or do not have the inclination for marriage. There are those eunuchs that have been physically castrated by others. Then there are those who have freely made themselves eunuchs. These eunuchs have foregone marriage in order to serve the kingdom.

My Unique (Eunuch) Path

I would say that this passage helps to describe the path I have taken in life. These three aspects of being a eunuch may help to illustrate certain points of my life. Looking back, I was like the person who was born as a eunuch. Perhaps, I already had received this "gift" of singleness. If so, I would have never known. Yet, I always wondered why I never had a girlfriend. Now, I wonder if this "gift" had always hindered me in relationships.

Then there are those who are made eunuchs by others. I could say that circumstances had forced me to become a eunuch. God had brought many girl friends into my life. But, they never could become girlfriends to me. There was just no one who was interested in me as more than a friend. So this "gift" of loneliness became more like a curse.

Then there are those who are eunuchs who renounce marriage for the sake of the kingdom. It was years later that I would find myself in this place. I had already found my vocation, but I still thought I was destined for marriage. At least God allowed me to understand what it means to have someone important to me. Then God allowed me to finally release these feelings. God was preparing me to fully embrace this gift of singleness. God was leading me to my lay single vocation. Then I was able to fully accept this mission.

"No trial has come to you but what is human. God is faithful and will not let you be tried beyond your strength; but with the trial He will provide a way out, so that you may be able to bear it" (1 Corinthians 10:13).

Finding My Way Out

I guess it's not surprising that this has always been my favorite Scripture. This passage really speaks to what I have gone through in my life. I was just living my life. Yet, it seemed as if I was facing one obstacle after another. My path was often complicated, filled with many vague twists and turns. The struggles and difficulties accumulated and snowballed into a path filled with adversity and no direction. I felt lost. Yet, God provided a way out for me. He allowed me to more fully encounter him by serving others. I found my place with a single lay vocation as an RE teacher.

Aside from Sunday Mass, I really did not have much of a faith life. While attending college, I worked weekends, frequently unable to go to Mass. After graduating, I was able to go back to Mass on a weekly basis. Yet, it took many years later for me to want to participate in Spiritual Growth, our young adult group. I found fellowship, but I still felt adrift in my loneliness.

It was years later that I was asked to help out with a high school RE class. I just wanted to focus my attention away from the struggles and difficulties I was facing. Little did I know that God was providing a way out for me. This began my journey into a deeper encounter with God.

So how can you encounter Jesus? You can find Jesus in serving others. You can find Jesus in reading Scripture. You can find Jesus at reconciliation. You can find Jesus in the Eucharist. You can find Jesus in the tabernacle. Whether you are silent, praying, or even crying out, give God your problem, so that He may provide a way out for you.

CHAPTER 36
FINAL THOUGHTS

Who Was She?

I couldn't very much tell my story without her being part of it. I felt it was important that I provide her with anonymity. She was a part of my life, but our paths only partly intersected. To be fair, we never had a dating relationship. I was attracted and interested in her. But, she couldn't reciprocate these feelings. It just wasn't meant to be. I always appreciated that she was always a good friend to me. But eventually, we went our separate ways. And I wish her the best.

I wrote this book for all my single peers who may question:
1. Why am I still single?
2. How do I deal with being single? (Alone or with God)
3. What is God's path for me?
4. Am I called to be single?

I am writing this in part to hopefully challenge other singles, who are also struggling in their attempts, to figure out their own path. At many times in my life, I have asked these questions. I imagine some singles may ask, "Why would you want to remain single?" That is a fair question.

I would say to you, "It is God's plan for me." And this is not just about me. I was beginning to see the bigger picture. If you knew where I came from, you'd know where I am today. I wrote this book to try to understand or make sense of my complicated path, filled with struggles, difficulties, obstacles, and ironies. And with God's help, I found myself where I am supposed to be. And I didn't see it coming!

Note from the author

Hi there! My name is Mike Szczesny. As we just live our daily lives, we encounter both the joys and struggles in life. It quite often becomes an adventure. Sometimes we know why we face these difficulties. And sometimes, God leads us down an unknown path. We all face these struggles. We all at some time or another must carry our struggles (crosses) on the path to which God leads us. But we are all in this together. And so in my struggles, God has led me down an unknown path to my becoming a catechist with a lay single vocation.

About the author

Mike Szczesny has been a Catholic catechist since 1993. He considers himselt to have a lay single vocation, which is directly tied to his vocation as a catechist. His interests include faith, doctrine, church history, scripture, exegesis, vocations, singleness issues and other topics. He is an accountant by profession and enjoys reading science fiction, playing chess, and partaking in hot sauces and peppers.

Szczesny hails from Texas where he strives to make learning about the faith fun and interesting. His blog site is "Resounding the Faith."

http://resoundingthefaith.com/

RESOUNDING
THE FAITH

About Leonine Publishers

Leonine Publishers LLC makes fine Catholic literature available to Catholics throughout the English-speaking world. Leonine Publishers offers an innovative "hybrid" approach to book publication that helps authors as well as readers. Please visit our web site at www.leoninepublishers.com to learn more about us. Browse our online bookstore to find more solid Catholic titles to uplift, challenge, and inspire.

Our patron and namesake is Pope Leo XIII, a prudent, yet uncompromising pope during the stormy years at the close of the 19th century. Please join us as we ask his intercession for our family of readers and authors.

Do you have a book inside you? Visit our web site today. Leonine Publishers accepts manuscripts from Catholic authors like you. If your book is selected for publication, you will have an active part in the production process. This book is an example of our growing selection of literature for the busy Catholic reader of the 21st century.

www.leoninepublishers.com

www.ingramcontent.com/pod-product-compliance
Lightning Source LLC
Chambersburg PA
CBHW031526040426
42445CB00009B/416